Praise for Stellar Presentations:

"I wish every entrepreneur would read it,"
                    --Robert Scoble, Startup Liaison Officer, Rackspace

"There have been a lot of books that attempt at helping entrepreneurs tell the story, but none provide the detail and examples needed to bring a presentation to life. Israel's masterfully shared his experiences working with some of the top entrepreneurs. Read the book once for enjoyment. Read the book again as a reference guide."

                -- R. Ray Wang, CEO Constellation Group

'This book is conversational and personal, allowing the rest of us to have a taste of Shel as our personal business coach.

While it gets into the nitty-gritty of presenting your new tech start-up … it offers tips that can be mapped to any sort of presentation you'll need to make on any subject on … any sort of public speaking."

                    --Chris Abraham, president Abraham Harrison LLC

"Geared for start-ups, Shel Israel packs a ton of practical wisdom into his new Kindle book …"

                    --Michael Markman, Brand Storyteller, MJ Markman Assocs.

"I just recommended Stellar Conversations to a company I am mentoring."
                                --Francine Hardaway

Also by Shel Israel

NAKED CONVERSATIONS: *How Blogs are Changing the Way Businesses Talk with Customers*

TWITTERVILLE: *How Businesses Can Thrive in the New Global Neighborhoods*

THE CONVERSATIONAL CORPORATION: *How Social Media is Changing the Enterprise*

Stellar Presentations
An Entrepreneur's Guide To Giving Great Talks

By Shel Israel

Dedication

To my grandkids: Samantha, Michael, Oliver and Isla. Also, to Grandma Jean, Brewster, Kinko and Paula, always Paula.

Contents

Introduction: But What if I Suck?

I was standing in front of a room filled with Indian entrepreneurs. The event was the annual NASSCOM Product Conclave, that country's largest gathering of startups and the people who care about them.

It looked like I'd be speaking to a half-empty room, but it turned out that Vinod Khosla, the luminary billionaire Indian-born American venture capitalist, was speaking in the room next door. When his session filled up, the overflow drifted in to the next closest venue where I was about to speak.

I was a bit apprehensive. This was my first visit to India. While, I have Indian friends in the San Francisco Bay Area where I live, this was different.

I was not yet sure I understood the culture of India. I had hoped to have a few days to glimpse the country before speaking there, but I had missed my original flight and barely got to Bangalore in time for my scheduled appearance.

So there I was in front of a room filled mostly with people who'd rather be listening to the hometown hero next door, covering a topic I had not previously talked about.

The lights were dimmed. A moderator said a few kind words and all eyes turned to me. A few seconds passed as we checked each other out.

I began by sharing a thought that had occurred to me as the room had filled up: "I've been assigned to talk about how to give a great presentation. This is scary. What if my presentation on great presentations sucks?"

A few people laughed. Then almost everyone joined in. Their faces went from neutral but curious to a look that said they were interested in what else I had to say.

I had made it to first base—or wherever Indians go when they get a hit in cricket, their sport of choice.

My talk went very well. When it was over, a small crowd gathered around me asking me questions. Some followed me out into the hallway. A few inquired about hiring me to consult or coach them.

I am still enjoying online conversations with people who saw that presentation and I've been invited to speak again next year. This is important because succeeding at a business-related presentation is merely a first step. The furthest you get is first base. I'll explain more about that later.

One outcome of that talk is this book. I realized that the majority of the people who came to see me speak were technology entrepreneurs. They were very well educated as engineers, but they knew little about the communications issues I covered.

The invitation to speak to startups about how to give great presentations made me realize how much I have learned on the topic over the past 30 years.

I came home to America thinking about the strategic importance of skillful presentations to startups, particularly at the critical moment when they are launching their company or flagship products.

So I decided to write *Stellar Presentations,* a small book for a niche market that I know and love. This is a book for tech entrepreneurs who need to present at conferences. I hope you find it useful.

I also hope that you find it fun. As I will explain, I believe fun is among the most vastly underrated of all business tools.

Throughout *Stellar Presentations*, I will share stories about speakers I have known, and why some of them remain fresh in my memory after many years and why some of them, well, memorably sucked. Please tell me what you think: email: shelisrael1@gmail.com . On Twitter, Facebook, Google Plus or LinkedIn, I'm shelisrael.

February 2012

Prologue: We Are Not Steve Jobs

Steve Jobs was the most stellar presenter the technology industry has ever produced. As technology industry presenters we have a great deal to learn from him.

But be careful. Studying Steve Jobs can also steer you wrong.

I saw him speak many times over the years. The most memorable of them goes back to the rainy Tuesday morning of January 24, 1984, when he introduced the Macintosh to the world.

When Jobs first walked out onto the stage at De Anza College's Flint Center in Cupertino, California there was an audible gasp from the audience.

The young entrepreneur had been famous for his hippie look. When he wasn't barefoot, he wore Birkenstock sandals. His hair and beard were in constant states of disarray; his clothes looked like they were overdue for a session with detergent.

But not on that day. On that rainy Tuesday morning, Jobs was clean-shaven and sported a stylish haircut. In short, he changed his own look and feel just as the Mac he was about to introduce would change the look and feel of personal computing.

But it was more than his apparel and hair that caused the audience to gasp. Jobs exuded a certain energy that would spread through the hall filled with about 1500 people. He showed on that day a presence that would inspire and captivate people in almost every room he ever entered.

Then there was his speaking style. He was candid and slangy. While other companies talked about the technology inside their gray boxes using the jargon of technical insiders, Jobs said the Mac was his baby and called it "insanely great."

His was the sort of language that Silicon Valley people used when chatting with friends in casual settings. It was the language that most people in the audience used when talking with each other.

He was what some speech coaches might call a natural. But, there really are no great naturals, just like no stars are really born overnight. To present so naturally, Jobs had practiced obsessively.

He also had the ability to look inward, find the most engaging parts of himself and serve them up to the audience in a way that sounded like he had thought it all up in that moment.

He was a maestro, getting from the audience what a symphony conductor might get from the string and percussion sections. On top of that he also played the magician. At the crescendo moment, Jobs picked up a mysterious black bag, and as if he were pulling a rabbit from a hat, he unveiled the first Macintosh as the audience gasped, then erupted in applause.

As twin spotlights centered on him and his new device, he tenderly set it on a table, connected it and pulled a floppy disk from his shirt pocket, inserting into the single external drive.

"My baby," he declared proudly, as the audience laughed and clapped even more.

Then he demonstrated what it could do "for the rest of us," those who did not have engineering or computer science degrees.

It turned out that Jobs had not really been the star of the show. He was just a very entertaining emcee. The Macintosh was the star and each of us immediately wanted one.

Now, the audience rose to its feet. People cheered; others applauded wildly. Even the press in the room, who were supposed to remain detached, joined in.

On that day, Steve Jobs broke the mold for technology presentations. Nearly every successful product intro that followed would borrow elements from what he did on that rainy Tuesday in 1984.

There were many variations.

Sometimes those launches would be accomplished at news conferences, but those were expensive and seemed to best suit large companies. Sometimes product introductions would be conducted via media tours where executives and their communications consultants would travel to New York City and Boston where the tech media was originally concentrated.

But over the years, more early-stage companies would introduce their products at conferences, where their products would be viewed and reviewed not just by the press and investors who would most certainly attend; but also by anyone and everyone who cared about technology products and companies.

In the tech sector these days, most companies launch in front of their peers at a multitude of product-focused tech conferences held all over the world.

In nearly 30 years, I have watched thousands of these product presentations. I have coached scores of entrepreneurs who have stood on the dais; many of them receiving best of show awards. I have also been the conference reviewer for the media. In short, I was the critic.

In all these experiences, I have not yet seen anyone who was as good at it as Steve Jobs was.

And that brings me to the warning. As a speaker, I have come to realize that even on my very best day, I will never be as good as Steve Jobs and as a coach, no one I help can ever aspire to eclipse him.

We are not Steve Jobs and we should not try to be.

It's rare than I can sit through a day of presentations without seeing one or more young entrepreneurs on stage wearing blue jeans and black turtlenecks.

If you are reading this book because you plan to launch your company with a Steve Jobs-like presentation, please heed this piece of urgent advice: Don't.

You are not Steve Jobs and imitating an original will not take you to where you want to go. Do not say "insanely great," or "one last thing," and choose any apparel you wish except jeans and black turtleneck.

At a recent conference I heard one member of the press once quip, "There are more Steve Jobs wannabees at these events than there are Elvis sightings in Las Vegas."

I've learned a good deal from studying Steve Jobs presentation. I use it in my presentations and in coaching others, but more than anything, I've learned that if you want to be stellar you must be original.

While we are not Steve Jobs, he was also not us. He was always smart enough not to imitate anyone. That is one of the many lessons we can learn from him.

There is much we can learn from other speakers, and I will talk about it shortly, but do not forget that what will make your talk really stellar is more likely to be found inside of you, rather than from someone who took the stage before you.

Part 1
Getting Ready

1. The Three Questions

I was raised as the youngest son in a Jewish family. That meant that each Passover I recited the ritual Four Questions that launched the story-telling part of our Passover dinner.

These days, I am rarely the youngest one at the table. But as a speaker and a coach, I begin the story that my clients or I will tell by reciting three questions:

1.   Who are the people in the audience?
2.   What do I have that they want?
3.   What do I want to accomplish by addressing them?

I ask the first two of these questions to conference producers. When they invite me. The third is mine to answer before I accept an invite.

Then, as happened in India, I replay the questions and the answers I received just before I start my talk.

Whatever your goal, you will come closer to achieving it if you understand who is listening to you and what you have that will interest them in some way related to their business.

I just told you how great Steve Jobs, was as a presenter, but, like most speakers, he had his off days. In one such case, it was clearly because he didn't understand what his audience wanted from him.

In 1997, shortly after taking the reigns of Apple for the second time, Jobs was presiding over a press conference, whose objective I do not recall. What was memorable, however, is that he was acting defensively and was evasive in answering direct questions. This made the reporters in the room increasingly aggressive.

Finally, he snapped. "I know you guys are out to get me, just like you were the last time." The room went quiet for a long moment.

Finally, Greg Zachary of the Wall Street Journal broke the awkward silence. "Steve, you have us all wrong," he said. "We don't care whether you win or lose. We just want a good story—and we get it either way."

People who attend a presentation are not there to serve the speaker's goals. They are there for their own business goals. Conversely, speakers are there to fulfill audience expectations.

Reporters want a good story. The recent college grads in your audience are looking for a good place to work. Consultants are looking for some new business to pitch, and so on down the line.

A presentation usually starts with the audience generally on the speaker's side. Other than hard-boiled reporters, most people will benefit far more if you succeed in telling them something that is useful or valuable to them.

When I'm speaking, I treat the audience as my customer. I try to give them what I have that they want. This is not altruism so much as a business strategy. Only by pleasing my audience can I subsequently achieve any of my own business goals.

If you represent a startup, the audience will be willing to cut you a little slack. They don't expect you to be as smooth as George Clooney accepting an award. They will forgive you a stutter or a stammer or even some minor typo in your slide deck. They will even forgive an occasional bug that pops up during your demo of a new product.

But this doesn't mean you are home free. The audience is yours to lose and there are many ways that can happen. You can be insufferably boring or ill-prepared; you can overstate your case, pretend to be someone you are not, or otherwise damage yourself by stretching credibility.

You can lose an audience by bad luck. Believe it or not, it is far better to follow a great speaker than one who puts attendees into nap mode. You might find yourself competing with a noisy lunch setup crew just outside your room or at the very worst; you can get caught in a lie.

I'll address these issues in upcoming chapters.

2. Watch Other Speakers

You can learn far more from speakers who have done what you are about to do than from just watching Steve Jobs.

It would help if you have already attended a conference that is like the one where you will be presenting. There's a lot to learn by observing.

When I go to a conference, I sometimes stand in the back of the room. It's useful to watch attendee computer screens. You can watch the points in a talk when users switch to activities other than listening and reporting on the speaker. Conversely, you can see when a good point is made and people start sharing it on their social networks.

If you cannot do that, then you have the benefit of digital archives. Almost every technology conference keeps an online library of previous speakers. Often, they show past presentation performances, spotlighting the best of show award recipients.

It is a good idea to watch the winners, but don't stop there. You can learn a ton, by watching a large block of videos. Awards often go to the most creative or theatrical of presentations but that might not be why you are speaking. You may be more interested in using the conference to make a deal, raise capital or find new talent. Achieving those objectives may shape a talk that will win no awards, but provide greater business benefit.

Pay attention to every detail. Were speakers dressed casually or did they wear suits or dresses? Where were the presentation screens located? Did speakers have to look away from the audience to see the screen when they were talking?

Take particular notice of the product demo if there is one. How soon did the speaker get to it? What percentage of the entire presentation is dedicated to the product? What other particulars of the company are shared with attendees?

I studied public communications in graduate school at Boston University. For me, the most memorable part of my studies was watching a video of the first televised presidential debate between John Kennedy and Richard Nixon.

Our professor made us study the debate in four modes:

1. Read the text. Before we even saw the debate, he required us to read the transcript at home. The next day, we talked about our impressions and voted on who won. The general consensus was that Nixon was victorious by a small margin.
2. Watch video only. Without sound, the class unanimous chose Kennedy. We agreed, he looked more like a leader and Nixon seemed "sweaty and shifty." [Later, we learned that Kennedy brought his own makeup artist and had used a sunlamp earlier in the day. By contrast, Nixon had banged his knee on a car door and was in serious pain. He also had allowed the studios to pack his face in pancake makeup, which dissolved badly in front of studio lights.]
3. Listen only. When we monitored an audio track, it was a close call but Nixon won the class consensus. He directly answered questions asked and seemed more knowledgeable in what he had to say.
4. Video & Audio. Again Kennedy won, and did so handily.

If my classroom was any indicator of the general public, Nixon would have beaten Kennedy hands down had the debate been held over radio rather than the new medium of television.

So when you present, you should keep in mind that what you say may not be the most memorable part of your presentation.

You are not running for president—at least not at this point in your career--and I certainly do not want you to finish this chapter feeling your words are unimportant in a presentation.

But when you watch the videos, pay attention to such details as pacing, gestures and body language. My guess is the ones you like the best were not the ones who spoke fastest.

3. Practice Obsessively

Practice may not make you perfect but it certainly makes you better. As I mentioned, Steve Jobs rehearsed obsessively for each of his presentations. It turns out that most of the great masters of any category do the same.

In Malcolm Gladwell's book, *Outliers,* he reported that the one thing the world's most successful achievers in art, entrepreneurship and sports shared in common was that each had practiced as many as 10,000 hours before they actually hit the big time. This was true for Bill Gates, Mozart and Canadian Hockey players.

Before most stars are "born overnight," they spend many nights and days practicing. They do it until they get it right, then they practice some more. I doubt that Mozart or Kobe Bryant or Michelangelo ever finished a practice, stepped back and said, "Well, that's good enough. Let's go have a beer."

I don't wish to overstate my point. You probably don't have time to practice 10,000 hours for your talk. Nor is the challenge before you quite as difficult as composing a Mozart masterpiece. But public speaking does require a lot of practice.

Talk in front of the mirror, with loved ones, with affectionate pets, and driving alone in your car. My dog Brewster loves whatever I say to him, so he builds my confidence. Thanks to Bluetooth, I no longer worry that I look crazy when I sit in traffic apparently chatting to my visor.

I'm a slow-but-dedicated distance runner. I find a good five-miler is the best place to practice a one-hour talk. It also reminds me to pace myself.

As a presentation coach, I will stick with a client, no matter what the barriers to success appear to be, but I will walk away from a deal, leaving income on the table, if someone simply tells me they are too busy to practice.

From my experience, the most common cause of presentation failure is a lack of preparation. The results are that instead of carrying the company and its product onto the playing field, a weak presentation becomes a new barrier for a young company, forcing it to undo the damage done.

That can be difficult. There is no second chance to make a great first impression.

There's one more aspect. You will need to script your presentation, indicating to the producer when the camera should be on you and when it should be focused on your product, or occasionally, a second speaker.

These scripts can deceive you. It takes only a short time to write a six-minute 900-word talk. (An average person will speak about 150-words-per minute to a group of 200 people.) But you will find that almost every time you rehearse it, you will want to edit something. Often my clients and I revise the script 20-30 times.

Once you've completed and rehearsed the script, the next step is to throw it away. In the end you don't want to sound like you are reciting overly scripted words.

All the rehearsing and rewriting will help immensely in understanding what you are going to say and in what order, but you need to sound as natural as if the words you've practiced 50 times were just being formed in your mind as you present.

4.   Your Positioning Statement

In the early 1980s, I worked for Regis McKenna, the man who Fortune Magazine in 1983 said, markets Silicon Valley. McKenna was widely acclaimed for his helping companies to find and articulate their positions and it was at the core of the public relations programs his agency used to put startups like Intel, Apple, Sun Microsystems and countless others onto the playing field.

I once attended a new business session in our firm's Palo Alto offices where a young and effervescent CEO was filling our conference room whiteboard with graphs and charts and bullet points about his start up.

He droned on about how his then-nonexistent product would evolve to change the world. As a team, we weren't quite sure whether or not the entrepreneur was exuding vision or suffering from hallucination.

McKenna let him talk on. When he finally stopped, our boss asked him how he planned to position his company.

Our entrepreneur jumped back up. "Great question! I'm glad you asked," he told us as he erased the whiteboard he had just filled.

"I have 42 possible positions," he proclaimed with pride, and then proceeded to write all of them on our white board. McKenna sat deadpan and the rest of us followed our boss's lead despite the fact that we were starting to feel that, like the characters in *Toy Story,* we were traveling to infinity and beyond.

Finally, our prospective client grinded to his completion. He sat down looking satisfied and awaited response from our resident positioning guru.

"Very interesting," McKenna responded. Then he gathered up his material to leave as we followed suit. From the conference room door he turned back to the CEO and said, "Pick one. Then get back to us."

It was a lesson I've carried with me for over 30 years. All too often, companies get lost in their own possibilities. They think a lot about what they *can* do without deciding what they *should* do. It is a serious problem. I have seen this lack of focus lead to many startup failures.

Similarly, I have witnessed many company presentations die a slow death on the dais through the same lack of focus. They meander

from point to point without making clear how these points are supposed to connect. Such talks may sometimes be entertaining. But when they are completed, attendees will walk away without a clear idea of the relevance of the new company and its product.

When I work with clients or on my own talks, I begin the process by developing a single, comprehensive positioning statement. It is stated early in the talk, and more important, it serves as an umbrella under which everything else must hang.

When I'm the speaker, I find my positioning statement is the compass that stops me from drifting off course. It determines the stories I tell in my talk and the key points each one needs to make.

My process runs contrary to the approach others use, particularly representatives of large, branded companies, who very often start a presentation with an outline that lists many 'talking points.'

If you are an early stage company, positioning your presentation is often a simple exercise that takes little time. It's about getting people aware and enthusiastic about your product. It's about telling attendees why they should care about what you are doing.

And it is expressed with jargon-free simplicity. I am not such an extreme minimalist as to suggest that you deliver your entire presentation in one sentence. But I do suggest you begin preparing your talk with your best thought on the topic at hand and that everything else you say supports or amplifies that overriding insight.

5. PowerPoint versus Storytelling

There are many ways to structure your presentation, but the two most common approaches center either on PowerPoint or storytelling. I heavily favor story telling.

Something there is that does not love a PowerPoint-dominated presentation. Conversely, we all seem to enjoy a good story.

PowerPoint can be tedious. Some presenters pack slides with data, graphs and text, which are often hard to read. Some speakers actually turn their backsides toward the audience, to read aloud from their slides. I don't advise it.

Because PowerPoint presentations can be so tiresome, a few conferences have banned their use. Conversely, other venues—particularly those geared to venture capitalists and angel investors require it.

I have to admit that I am a little schizophrenic about PowerPoint myself. It was among the first products SIPR launched, when we helped the developers introduce it back in 1987. When I speak, I sometimes share that fact with audiences. Then I beg their forgiveness. It always gets a laugh.

Despite its flaws and frequent abuses, PowerPoint can add significant value to a talk when it is not misused. Many of the most stellar talks I've seen have incorporated PowerPoint or some other slide software.

I always use Powerpoint in my presentations. One of my dirty little secrets is that without it, I am likely to lose my place while speaking.

But there's another reason to include it. PowerPoint can be a great supplement to your talk. I use it to illustrate the stories I tell in the same way photos enhance the articles and blogs I publish.

I'm a minimalist on text. If I use bullet points, there are usually only one-to-five words per bullet and the font is large enough to read from the back of the room.

When I click to a new slide, I pause and let people view it for a moment. When their eyes return to me, I start talking and I move in front of my slide so that I don't get upstaged by it.

The core of nearly all my presentations is telling stories that illustrate business points. It has been my experience that story-based presentations are infinitely more memorable than PowerPoint-centric talks.

Stories are part of our human DNA. Our culture, religion and national history are based on stories, not bullet points. There are stories with us today that were first told in five minutes time 5,000 years ago.

By contrast, I have seen quite a few PowerPoint slides that felt like it took 5,000 years to present and were remembered for less than five minutes.

I bet when you get together to enjoy a meal or perhaps just an adult beverage with your friends, you share a few good stories.

But, have you ever shared a good PowerPoint slide over a beer with a pal? I didn't think so.

Part 2
In the Room

6.   Save Your Best for First

Steve Jobs sometimes rambled on for over two hours. Then, just as the audience thought his presentation was about to trickle to an uneventful close, he'd pause and say "one last thing …". Then he'd deliver a surprise show-stopping announcement that brought the house down.

Those three words became so much a part of his presentation signature, that in 2011, PBS produced a documentary on him that they called it *One Last Thing.*

I'm not Steve Jobs, and in all my experience, I've witnessed no other speaker besides him who could ramble on even for two minutes. People either hop on the web or stroll out of the room.

If you are presenting at a startup conference, you may have as little as five or six minutes, so you have scant time to waste. You need to cut to the chase quickly.

There's a structure called "inverted pyramid." Every journalism student learns about it in his or her introductory newswriting courses.

In paper-based publishing, editors often assigned a reporter to write a story that fit a particular news hole. Reporters usually could not

resist the temptation to write a little longer. So editors simply measured the copy and chopped it off at the bottom to fit, often without even reading the part they were deleting.

The inverted pyramid structure ensures that the juiciest part of the story gets published, while the lesser tidbits may not.

As a speaker, your constraint is not space, but time. The inverted pyramid structure will also work for you. It disciplines you to get your best points out at the top. If you find that you are running short of time, then you can comfortably chop out the lesser details before reaching your deadline.

It is a far smarter strategy than some speakers use. When they see they are coming to the end of their allotted time they talk faster. Some are foolish enough to waste precious seconds complaining about not having enough time.

If you are giving a talk as short as five or six minutes, you'll want to make every second count. If the conference introduces you by name or company, or if there is a slide that shows who you are and who you represent, then don't waste time by repeating your introduction. Every second may count, but you will lose big points if you rush through your presentation.

You need to tell your best story in a short period, yet you need to be just a little entertaining and above all you must remain credible in everything you do or say.

So be smart. Save your best for first, and let your talk end with a next step, which very often is telling people where they can see your demo at the conference or how they can download your beta online.

7.   Your Product is Your Star

There are many conferences that are mostly about startups such as TechCrunch Disrupt, the Launch Conference and DEMO. These top-tier events can attract well over a thousand participants from all over the world. There are also hundreds of startup and product get-togethers all over the world each year.

Attendees have diverse interests except for one thing—they are all looking for new technologies. The common thread that ties all these people in all these gatherings together is product. That is what the people in front of you want to know about.
More specifically, they want to know what your product can do for them.

So don't worry about grandiloquence. Most entrepreneurs have more passion and talent related to products than they do for speechmaking.

So when I tell you to save your best for first, very often that will be your product demo, which is as much the star of your show as the Mac was for Jobs back in 1984. You are the host-moderator, just as he was for the Mac.

Don't meander or pontificate. Get your demo going within 30 seconds. And once again, use the inverted pyramid to structure the demo as well as your overall presentation.

Get to the "wow" feature first. Then the rest of your talk will be cake. In fact, once you elicit your wow, some of what you say next may get lost because members of your audience are busy sharing their enthusiasm online.

This is the good news.

The bad is that sometimes during a demo you may face an unwanted surprise. In addition to serving as your product's emcee, you also need to be prepared to serve as its understudy.

Chances are you will be using the web in a conference hall while hundreds of people are using the same wifi connection at the same time. Not only that, but you will be showing a product that has not yet been fully tested.

Very few tech conferences come off without at least one wifi crash, and that bug your team stayed up all night to fix may unfortunately reincarnate itself onstage in the middle of your talk.

How do you anticipate such things and what do you do when they happen?

First, resist the urge to fly solo. Many CEOs like to do the demo themselves. That's fine in lots of circumstances but it increases the risk factor during a conference launch demo.

It's safer to have one or two members of your tech team do the driving while you continue to do the talking. If something technical goes wrong, they can work on it, while you continue to address the audience. If they cannot fix the problem you might keep a canned mockup handy. Make it clear that you are not doing a live demo, but let attendees see what it would have looked like.

Glitches happen. The challenge is to maintain what Hemingway called "grace under pressure." Let the audience see your cool.

The best example that I recall happened years ago when DEMO was the pre-eminent tech product conference. A CEO was doing quite

well with his own demo, when about halfway though, the connection crashed and the audience found themselves staring at his computer desktop on the big screen.

The speaker smiled and never lost a beat. He quipped, "Well, would you like to see my accounts payable ledger?"

As we chuckled, he said. "Let me tell you how great it would have been," and then, at a relaxed pace, he described what we would have seen had the demo worked.

He then invited attendees to visit the company's kiosk in the product pavilion later in the day, "to see the performance that the demo gods didn't dare to let you see here."

Attendees felt his pain, and admired his humor. They visited his demo station and liked what they saw. They talked about him and his company during lunches and in hallway chatter. He went on to receive a Demo God Award.

It's best, of course, to have your product work as intended when the spotlight shines upon it in center stage. It doesn't always go that way. Always have a plan B and even a Plan C.

The way you recover will say a great deal about you, your team and your company.

8. Jerry Kaplan Tossed a Notepad into the Air …

Have you every heard of Rube Goldberg? He would have had a field day satirizing some of the charts and graphs you may have suffered through in presentations: The ones that ignored the inverted pyramid structure and tried to pack too much complex information into too small a space.

Rube Goldberg was a very famous political cartoonist in the middle of the last century. His work appeared in many of the most popular newspaper editorial pages.

His recurring theme was to create wildly complex mechanical devices that performed brain-dead simple tasks. For example, the little guy who starred in many of Goldberg's cartoons would be seated alone at a large dining table. A complicated apparatus occupied almost the entire table except where he sat. Its function was to cool a single spoonful of soup.

Goldberg's satire hit home during an era when people were becoming concerned with the bureaucracy of a military industrial complex that was becoming unnecessarily unwieldy.

His work earned him a Pulitzer Prize. Webster Dictionary listed "Rube Goldberg" as an adjective describing "inane complexity."

Let me use it as a verb: Don't Rube Goldberg your audience.

Keep your talk, your demo and your slides as simple as possible.

Sometimes new entrepreneurial speakers often go in the opposite direction. They want people to understand how difficult their software was to make.

But people don't care about that. They want to know how simple your product is to use, and how it solves a problem they recognize.

There is a principle of logic called "Occam's Razor," which states that the simplest solution is the best. The Shel Israel Speaker's corollary to it is: The most stellar presentations are the simplest.

The simplest presentations attract the most customers and generate the most press coverage. They are the most memorable and they generate the most conversation.

There are many good examples, but let me give you one that has endured 25 years. It involves a startup company in a presentation situation that can be even more daunting than the conference launch presentation: the investor pitch.

Jim Collins told a story in his popular business book *Good to Great*.

In 1987, Jerry Kaplan and a few high-profile technologists co-founded a startup called Go Corp.

They had a big idea. Go Corp. would invent the first tablet computer. You would enter data with a pen-like stylus that wrote on the glass face of the thin portable device.

It would be as simple as writing with a pen on a notepad—but extremely complex to develop, design and build.

The time came to get financing. Kaplan was already well-known and thought he would get started by going around to talk informally with a few investors he knew to measure interest and to get input before he actually wrote his business plan.

That brought him to Palo Alto-based Kleiner Perkins Caufield & Byers, the legendary Silicon Valley venture firm. He showed up expecting to have an off-the-record chat, but it turned out he was one of several entrepreneurs scheduled to make formal presentations to the firm's partners.

Kaplan was unprepared. He thought of walking out, but then he would be turning his back on a huge opportunity. He decided to go ahead and take the risk.

He had no PowerPoint, no prototype, not even an artist's rendering of what this 'never-before' computer would look like. His tech team was not with him and he had nothing to demonstrate.

He was still weighing his options when his name was called.

Kaplan walked in and faced a large square conference table. Seated around three sides were some of the best-known and most formidable investors of the time.

He waited for quiet. All eyes were upon him.

Without saying a word, he took the blue-lined paper notepad he was using to take notes and tossed it into the air. It arched, and then fell with an audible slap onto the conference table.

"This is my model for the future of personal computing," he declared.

It was a simple message. The future of computing would be in handheld portable devices. Go's vision was that it would look and feel very much like the ubiquitous legal notepad most business people used in 1987.

The Kleiner folk were stunned at first, but they got the simple, powerful message. At the end of the day, there is only one message you need to deliver to smart investors and you don't need the usual props: "Rich. This product will make you very, very rich."

Jerry Kaplan's notebook sailing in the air was a presentation positioning statement. Kaplan didn't talk about the challenges of building the first pen input operating system. He did not talk about weight, or industry standards or any of the myriad issues his team would have to deal with.

Those issues were raised as the questions began. The Kleiner Perkins folks drilled like a dentists on steroids. Kaplan answered what he could.

Shortly thereafter, Go Corp. got its term sheet.

And it all happened because Kaplan delivered a single, simple sentence to the right audience at the right time.

9.   The 'Tell-Me-More' Strategy

"OK," you may be thinking, "I get the simple part."

But can't you take it too far? If you say too little, won't it seem like you're poorly prepared or have a half-baked idea?"

You can take anything too far, and, of course, you can err by over-simplifying. You do not want to fill a six-minute slot with a one-minute presentation and forget about tossing notebooks into the air. It's been done.

When you present, you need to make judgment calls on everything you include or omit. I advise you to follow my mother's refrigerator rule: When it doubt, throw it out.

It is stronger to err on the side of simplicity over complexity. It is far better to finish early in your talk than rush to beat the buzzer.

If you watch the online videos of DEMO, the Launch Conference and Techcrunch Disrupt, you will notice that almost every winner finishes comfortably before the time limit expires.

There's a reason and it's not always the obvious one: it takes more time to make your talk shorter than it does to let it go longer. It takes more time to think through a simple graphic than it does to befuddle the audience with Rube Goldberg schematic.

In Chapter 2, I asked you to think about three questions when you begin work on your presentation: 'Who are these people? What do I have that they want? And what do I want to accomplish by addressing them?'

There's a follow up question, one that also shapes the strategy of your talk: What do you want them to do next?

I also referred earlier to the audience collectively as your customer.

I emphasize the word 'collectively' and I use the singular for 'customer,' to make a point. If you see them each as a prospect, then you will step into the trap of cluttering your talk with the diverse information that may interest an investor, future hire, editor, a business partner and so on. You'll end up Rube Goldberg-ing your presentation into a muddled, disjointed mess.

The trick is to find a common thread. Focus on the points that will interest almost everyone.

You will be unwise if you try to get attendees to know everything they should know about you, your team, your business model, the people you hope to hire, your end game, ad nauseum in the short time allotted to your talk.

Instead, just whet their appetites. After you you're done, you want people to approach you with a specific request: "Tell me more."

You can spend the rest of the conference going as narrow and as deep as attendees relevant to your business want you to go.

Your talk is a monologue. It succeeds when it spurs conversations. And those conversations can help your company go many places that it needs to reach.

Besides, the feedback you get after your talk will help you to make course corrections based on input from people who matter to your company.

10. Come as You Are

When blogging first started to catch on in business, Dave Winer, who created and evangelized the new way of communicating, advised content authors to "come as you are."

What he meant was that people shouldn't worry about an occasional grammar gaffe or typo. Such flaws in your published work demonstrated your authenticity. It showed that there was a real person speaking, not some official corporate spokesperson.

I think it remains good advice for bloggers today and I think the advice holds true for startup presentations.

We tend to trust "people like us." Richard Edelman, head of the world's largest independent PR agency conducts an annual "Trust Barometer" poll and in several recent years, he found people trust those who look, feel and sound like they do, rather than polished business people or actors or professional athletes.

The painful irony is that people who sound like you and me, often get on the stage and try to sound like someone entirely less trustworthy.

I have watched a friend, who is filled with a passion and contagious candid style, step onto the dais for his company presentation and suddenly sound like a Fox newscaster.

It was like he assumed a secret identity.

Here are some of the afflictions different speakers suffer:

- Pedantic professor syndrome. For some reason, perfectly articulate people start talking like they were lecturing in a classroom on Pleistocene geology. They lull you to sleep by using words you've never heard and quoting philosophers you've never read.

When small words like "use," are replaced with longer words such as "utilize" that mean precisely the same thing, it's a big hint that there's a pedantic professor onstage.

Big words don't make you sound smarter—just duller.

- Jargon. Every industry has its insider language. You may have to introduce a word or two and you should briefly define them for the outsiders in the room. Use too many and you will lose everyone except the insiders.

- Clichés. These are first cousins to jargon. But instead of using a term no one has heard, you use one everyone has heard too many times before.

   A few of the most senior clichés include, 'all new,' 'imagine… ,' 'It's really that simple… ,' and, of course, 'If you're like me … .' Such phrases have worn thinner than the Arctic ice cap.

- Artificial costuming. Presenters worry a lot about attire. At tech conferences, it's less important than you may think. Just make sure your clothing is not distracting or outrageous. I try to dress similar to attendees, but one click up, to imply that I consider addressing them to be important.

My first consideration is comfort. I almost never wear something I have not worn before, and I never wear garments that don't feel like a perfect fit. I want clothing that feels like an old friend and lets me move around without having to smooth or adjust anything.

I'm comfortable in a suit, but hate neckties. The only way you will get me to wear one is at a formal event.

Clothing is part of the first impression you make as you walk on stage, but then it should fade into the background as you speak and introduce your product. Choose apparel that supports you without threatening to upstage you.

Besides, people rarely remember what you wore after the event unless you selected something outrageous. Don't choose anything that will compete with you for attention.

A few examples:

- <u>Shoes that click or clack</u>. It is wisest if the audience never notices anything about your footwear. If their attention is down there, they may be missing your words or product demo. Shoes that have taps or tassels are a speaker liability.

  Women very often pick high heel shoes that may make them look great. But if they cause any difficulty in walking, or standing still for an extended period, they can hurt a presentation.

- <u>No moving experiences</u>. Likewise, when you are presenting, you need to be sure that you are wearing nothing that jingles, jangles, swings, sways or otherwise distracts.

- <u>Stay solid</u>. If your talk is to be video recorded, patterned clothing—particularly checks and small plaids may appear to be in independent motion, causing a distraction for viewers. It's wisest to go solid.

- <u>Be cool</u>. One important little factoid: the temperature is often set to make the room feel comfortable to a seated attendee.

But you will be standing and heat rises. If you are standing
on the same floor as where your audience is sitting, your
head will be one degree warmer than theirs, because it is
higher up. If you are standing on a stage, it could be as much
four degrees warmer. While attendees watch you in comfort,
you may start perspiring in a most unappealing way. See if
you can ask the producer to set the room temperature down a
little bit.

- <u>Find friendly faces</u>. It is important to engage the audience
  and this involves both body language and eye contact.
  Frequently, speakers are advised to look into the eyes of
  attendees. But there could be hundreds of them and it
  becomes impractical.

When I start to speak I look for one friendly face in each section of
the room and my eyes move from one perceived supporter to the
next. It creates the illusion that I have great eye contact when, in
fact, I've looked at only a few people.

11. Passion versus Polish

The opening words in the book I co-authored with Robert Scoble, *Naked Conversations* were, "We live in a time when most people don't trust large organizations."

Among the reasons we cited is that representatives for large organizations seem to talk in a strange and duplicitous language that real people don't use.

We called it "corpspeak," a nomenclature that is written by enterprisewide committees. Marketing folks insert messages and adjectives they think will pump up excitement. Lawyers add confusing phrases so that Marketing's hype doesn't get the company sued. Branders insert corporate ID to ingrain on people's mind the company's image in the same way ranchers use branding irons on cattle buttocks.

Representatives of the same enterprise sound remarkably like each other when they present and their slides appear to be crafted by the same hands. We are supposed to be left with the impression that a few hundred thousand employees residing in 150 countries and speaking multiple languages all sing in perfect harmony with each other and march together in lockstep.

Obviously, those who coach enterprise speakers are using a different playbook from this one.

In fact, they would disagree with almost everything I have advised you to do so far. They would prefer to script your every gesture and every word.

It isn't that I am wrong or that they are right. It is that when it comes to presentations, one size does not fit all. What I advise you here is designed for representatives of early stage companies.

Shel Holtz, a fellow author, speaker and communications consultant says the difference can be summarized as "passion vs. polish."

"There's nothing wrong with being polished in your presentation. Knowing just when to advance a slide, having your gestures down pat, avoiding the dreaded 'ummm.' They're all going to make your presentation more watchable."

"But large corporation presentations have aspects that go beyond solid preparation. The slides use corporate templates and the patter is laden with corporate jargon," Holtz told me.

"Conversely," he said, "Small businesses and startups are hungry, and their best spokespeople reflect a certain passion by incorporating unbridled enthusiasm into their presentations. Nothing is more compelling than watching a true believer make her case."

The first clue that you are about to be doused in corpspeak comes when the presenter refers to himself in the corporate "we," rather than the personal "I."

Some startup speakers try to position their companies as bigger than they really are. They present with more polish than passion and with

slides that appear manufactured by central casting. That sort of stuff leaves most entrepreneurial audiences ice cold.

Someday you may be an officer in a public company and your advisers may convince you that you must suffer the curse of the living corpspeakers. But don't try to get there too soon.

Songwriter Don McLean described America's greatest living lyricist, Bob Dylan as having "a voice that came from you and me."

Try to find a voice that represents you and your audience. Talk to them as you would a professional friend.

12. Personalize

In addition to saying "I" instead of "we," and relying on stories to make your point, you need to insert yourself into your presentation.

One of my early PR experiences was with Robert Carr, who was chief scientist at the late Ashton-Tate, then the world's third largest software company. Carr would later be inventor of the pen-input software at Go Corp., which he co-founded and go on to a successful career at Autodesk.

I helped Carr introduce Framework, one of the first integrated software packages. I started to learn about the power of storytelling from him.

As we visited press and analysts, Carr began on a personal note. He didn't list his past achievements or where he went to college. He didn't explain about Ashton-Tate's market research or demographic targets. Instead, he talked about a personal problem.

He told editors and analysts that the software of the day, didn't allow him to work the way he liked to work. He liked to jump around from one topic or task to another. Back then, when you could only run one software application at a time, this was time-consuming, and often frustrating.

So Framework, Carr explained, let you toggle from spreadsheet to word processing and even into graphics and then back without having to close one software program and open another.

This may sound obvious in today's world, but at the time it was world changing.

As the PR guy monitoring the conversation, I would watch each editor get drawn in. Their heads would nod and they would interject that they shared that problem, which is just about as good as it gets in a media interview.

Carr generated great coverage. More than that, he ignited relationships with editors that remained with him through a long and successful career.

Carr got up close and personal at a time when it was unfashionable. Instead of positioning himself as an official corporate spokesperson, he presented himself just as a geek with a problem that he solved for himself and now he wanted to share it with others.

Whether your audience is an editor or a room full of your professional colleagues, discussing your professional problems and how your product helps solve them is among the most successful tactics I know.

Framework is an old story, recalling times that seem quaint when viewed from today's cloud-based perspective. Much of our personal lives, interaction and entertainment have migrated onto the Internet.

Take photos for example. When I was helping Carr extol the virtues of integrated software most people were storing memories of their most precious moments onto colored pieces of paper called photos. We stored them in paper albums and in boxes that filled closets and garages.

These 'Kodak moments' remained the state of the art until about the turn of the century.

By 2006, most new photos were digital. Instead of closets and garages, we stored them on our computers and online services.

But a major problem from the old days carried over into the new digital age. We could never find the photos we wanted without spending more time than we had.

Munjal Shah started a company to solve that. His company was called Riya, after his daughter.

I went in to see if I could help him prepare a presentation to launch his company at an upcoming DEMO Conference. We sat in his conference room. He had a PowerPoint deck at the ready, but he began just by talking to me.

"I have 36,245 photos in my digital collection," he told me. "Each is named something like IMG_3712.JPG." Then he turned on his slides. The first was of an adorable two-year-old child.

"That's my daughter. Her name is Riya. Isn't she cute?" He waited for my answer, which was affirmative, of course.

Then he went on to talk about how his new company would let you recognize anyone in your photo collection. If Shah tagged his daughter in just one photo, his new online software would then identify all photos of her in his collection.

In less than five minutes I was hooked. In my coaching, I encouraged him to present at DEMO precisely as he had presented to me. He did. It worked and he received a DEMO God Award.

Telling a story about yourself that solves a problem others have is very often the shortest distance between you and your audience.

Better still, chances are good that you already know how to tell that story. You have already shared it a few times with friends and family. Now all you have to do is practice a lot so that you tell it extremely well when it matters most.

13. Share your dream

I've counseled you a lot to stay away from hype and buzz, fibs and fabrications. Please do not interpret that as a license for mediocrity. Being dull can cost you dearly. The trick is to know how to stir the audience without losing authenticity. For a good startup, this may be easier than you think.

When you think about it, startups are built on dreams and dreams can be memorable and even inspirational. If you have elected to be an entrepreneur, then you are willing to take risks to make your dreams come true. That's exciting.

Not only do people love a good story, they are particularly fond of the ones where an underdog with a dream struggles to overcome formidable obstacles--and then succeeds in the wildest ways imaginable.

So you can use all that stuff about seeing a market opportunity to explain your company and product, but somewhere in all that MBA-type talking there is a vision and sharing it will put more people on your side faster and keep them there longer than any business model or graphic rendering.

Dreams make the great stories that endure for many years. Alexander Graham Bell got burned with acid and his assistant heard him through the telephone that had not previously worked. Scott Cook saw his wife getting frustrated with the family checkbook at the kitchen table, and then founded Intuit.

Bell and Cook started with visions. The visions became stories and from there enduring companies emerged.

Dave McClure, a Silicon Valley angel investor, is a frequent judge at conference startup presentations. His most frequent comment to a presenting entrepreneur is, "I just don't see your passion."

While I think McClure is sometimes too harsh, he makes a good point. Stellar performances are built on passion and dreams. Share them with your audience and they will want to help you make your entrepreneurial dreams come true.

Part 3
Intangibles

14. Why Credibility is Like Virginity

I mentioned earlier that most people who attend startup conferences are a forgiving lot.

But there are limits. They will not tolerate deliberately misleading statements; omissions of a relevant fact; or plain, old-fashioned, bold-faced lies.

In the heat of your presentation moment, make certain that you do nothing to damage your credibility. It is very much like virginity. Once you lose it, then it's pretty much gone.

We live in an age when everyone is a fact-checker. Even while you are still delivering your presentation, people in the audience—or those connected to them—are already checking other sources on claims that you made.

Someone should have told Joe Nacchio.

He was CEO-Chairman of a telephony company called Qwest Communications. In 2002, he was speaking at PC Forum, then one of technology's most prestigious conferences.

Blogging was just then coming into fashion and several of the most prominent bloggers were attending PC Forum. They were live blogging as Nacchio delivered his keynote.

Nacchio was edging close to the SEC limits on forward-looking statements. He contended that Qwest's recently battered stock was being unjustly hammered and would soon rebound.

As he spoke, bloggers in the room were relaying his statements in near real-time. Attendees were following the novelty of instant recaps and adding comments. Elsewhere in the world people who could not attend the conference joined in on the conversation. For them, it was the next best thing to being there.

One of them was Buzz Bruggeman, an entrepreneur who was following from his North Florida offices. Bruggeman did something traditional journalists are supposed to do.

He started checking other sources. At Yahoo!Finance he discovered that in recent weeks Nacchio had sold off about $200 million in shares of his own Qwest stock, the same stock he was touting from the dais.

Bruggeman relayed this back to the bloggers in the room, who in turn, posted what he had uncovered. Attendees started adding decidedly unfavorable comments about the speaker in front of them.

At about that point, PC Forum Host-Producer Esther Dyson recalled later, "The audience seemed to grow hostile."

Nacchio was caught in a lie. It happened before he knew it and it became a watershed moment in his career, which would soon dramatically plummet.

In the ensuing months, an SEC investigation led to Nacchio being arrested and convicted of insider trading. He was sentenced to six years, fined $19 million, and had to repay over $50 million in profits he had made through illegal trades.

Qwest eventually went bankrupt and was then acquired by a company that now provides low-cost Internet connections. The story came back into the news in 2011, when Nacchio sued his lawyers for overcharging him and padding an expense account with items that included purchasing underwear.

It's reasonable to assume Nacchio would have been indicted anyway, even if he had not spoken at PC Forum.

But look at the speed by which his misleading statements were detected. You may be the last speaker in a long day at a third tier event, but when you speak from a stage these days, you have to assume that anyone in the world could be listening in and somewhere someone will check out your assertions.

Even the smallest fib is like a loose thread in the fabric of your talk. It may get pulled and everything will unravel.

15. The 'Little Guy' Advantage

There are certain advantages to being small. Joe Fernandez has used them very much to the advantage of Klout, the company he founded and heads up.

Klout claims it can measure your social network's influence, but many people disagree, including me.

When I wrote negatively about the company, I was surprised and a little flattered that Fernandez tweeted me an invitation to lunch. When we met up, I argued that Klout was measuring something of value, but it just wasn't what I would call influence.

I was prepared for a hot debate, but Joe disarmed me by agreeing. He conceded that I might be right. Then he smiled, shrugged and said, " Hey, don't pick on us! We're just a little start up! Give us a chance to figure it all out."

Then he explained the great complexity of how Klout derives its numbers and he clued me in to the company's strategy. Klout aspires to serve social media in the way Nielsen serves television. The TV pollster provides a single number by which one program can be compared in popularity to another.

Klout is measuring *something*. It's hard to describe just what that is, but I could not find a better word to describe it than influence. If these ratings were coming from a large and established entity I might have found myself predisposed to continuing my assault on the influence claim. But like most people, I tend to cut little guys some slack.

When you present, my advice is to use the little guy position for as long as you can.

You may aspire to eliminate Facebook or Google, but there is no need to make that claim. Instead you can point to the smaller problem your fledgling product is solving in its earliest phases.

You do not have to claim that you already know what customers want when you have very few customers. But if you show that you are both humble and tenacious, people will stay on your side.

In fact, that approach helped Google, who simply aspired at first to be a better form of free search and Facebook, which was just a service to help Ivy League fraternity brothers find attractive dates on campus.

As Google and Facebook have proven—and Apple as well—you can go a very long distance before people wake up and discover that you are now one of the big guys.

Besides sympathy, the little guy profile will keep you off the larger competitor's radar at least for a while. You really don't want to piss off the gorillas until you have gained strength and momentum. When you just edge your way onto the playing field, you want your larger rival to ignore you—at least until you can poke it in the eye..

The little guy advantage can be strategically powerful if you do not blow it by making huge claims, such as that you will destroy your category-leading competitor.

Startup cemeteries are filled with young dreamers whose assets include money from friends and family, five employees, a few computers and no customers. Yet they proclaimed to the world how they would replace Facebook, Google, Microsoft or IBM.

None of them succeeded. But the tragedy is that they really never had to. All they had to do is keep delivering new products to customers. In the end, the market decides if you will take down the giants in your sector, and there's a tendency for them to support you more passionately and with greater tolerance when you are still perceived as just a little guy.

16. Lethal Generosity

I introduced the concept of Lethal Generosity in my 2009 book, *Twitterville*. To describe how it works, let me share a couple of my favorite examples.

Jeremiah Owyang is a founding partner in Altimeter Group, the leading social analyst consultancy. Today, he's a certified luminary, but when I first met him he was a hard-working, mid-level grunt at Hitachi Data Systems [HDS]. Based in Silicon Valley, HDS is a subsidiary of the Japanese conglomerate and a leader in enterprise data storage.

Owyang was the huge company's only employee dedicated to social media, and he kept fighting uphill to get his organization to use conversational media more effectively.

He came up with a great idea: He created an online forum and invited everyone who had an interest in the topic to join in: users, media, analysts, partners, and vendors.

He gave it a very generic—and intentionally forgettable—name: the Data Storage Wiki. So everyone wound up calling it the Hitachi Wiki. After all, they were the one's who started it and they were investing money to store and host it.

The wiki generated good attention in the data storage community. More interestingly, it caused a real dilemma for Hitachi's competitors. Here was Hitachi extending an invitation to collaborate and solve customer problems.

This was lethal to competitors. If they declined, then they would appear to not be interested in helping customers solve problems. If they agreed, they would be seen as following Hitachi's thought leadership. If they opted to build their own for their existing customers, then they were obviously building a walled city that was of less benefit to their customers.

Let's look at another case.

In 2008, the City of Toronto announced it could no longer afford to continue the tradition of keeping public transportation running throughout the night on New Year's Eve in the interest of public safety.

Beer maker Molson Coors immediately stepped up to the plate, announcing that as an example of its commitment to 'responsible drinking', it would contribute half the money the City had withdrawn and called upon other Canadian companies to make up the difference.

Specifically, they urged LaBatts, their leading Canadian competitor to join them.

How could LaBatts refuse? If they did, would it mean they supported irresponsible drinking, or that they didn't care about public safety? But if they joined in, they were following their rival's thought leadership.

As a Little Guy, you can use Lethal Generosity concepts in your presentations with devastating results. It can create the perception of moral superiority to your larger competitor and it can force them to respond, when they would greatly prefer to publically ignore you.

Pick an issue that is important to your customers: Internet privacy or piracy, child safety, clean water, sustainable energy or some other challenging issue that elicits both passion and conversation and make it a key component of your presentations. Declare the formation of an online community, a fundraising campaign or some activity in which you can engage customers toward a common cause. Promise to give a certain percentage of your revenue to a worthy cause.

Then invite your larger competitor to join you in supporting the cause like Molson Canada did in Toronto. That competitor will face the same two choices—ignore your invitation and not join customers in achieving a common cause, or joining in the effort, thus positioning you as their thought leader.

Either way your generosity to customers and the world can be lethal to your competitor.

And there's a second part to it. The more you give to an audience the closer you get. And the closer you get to them, the more difficult it is for a competitor to get in between the two of you.

17. Bring the Whole Gang

Most of this book has looked at what happens at the podium. After all, it is about startups making stellar presentations.

If this is all you look at, then you might opt to bring only yourself and whoever will staff your demonstration stations. After all, these are tough economic times and early-stage companies are almost always financially constrained.

However, just looking at your time at the podium may give you a myopic perspective, and not taking as many team members to the conference could very well prove to be penny wise and dollar foolish.

You'll be speaking for just a few minutes and the events related to the conference will go on from 1-3 days. There may be a golf tournament or other social event before the conference actually starts. There are lunches and dinners and occasional Karaoke performances. There is an exhibition area. There are all sorts of business conversations going on in quiet nooks of the hotel or conference center.

Every square inch of the venue and any single moment may hold a surprise business opportunity. I once landed a speech coaching deal while waiting in the men's room line at a TechCrunch Disrupt.

My point is simple: the more members of the team that you bring to the party the more business opportunities you will have, the more your company's name will be noticed, the more people will understand that there is a team behind your logo.

And the advantages of bringing more people are two-way. Not only do you get to have more mouths getting the word out on your behalf, you also have more ears taking information in.

The more team members at the conference the more business intelligence you gather that you can later share and use internally.

There's one more advantage to bringing the whole team: morale. For months your staff has been working long, hard hours in preparation for this conference. Without their contributions, your products, collateral materials, exhibit area and your media appointments just wouldn't be what they are.

It can be demoralizing to a team that has worked so hard for so long to be left at home as the curtain goes up at a big event. Conversely, seeing public reaction to their work can motivate and energize the team.

18. The Secret of Cantaloupe

Someone once declared that God is in the details. On the speaking circuit, the Devil lurks there too.

When I'm a scheduled speaker I bring a little emergency preparedness kit with me. And through personal experiences, I've learned how to manage several many unwanted surprises. Let me share a few you may unfortunately find yourself facing.

- The secret of cantaloupe. My voice just isn't as strong as it should be. If I speak for over 30 minutes straight, it starts to crackle.

  This happened to me during a book launch presentation in Toronto. Painfully CBC, the national TV network was recording as I started sounding a bit like a frog with laryngitis.

  After I came to my embarrassing conclusion, a woman approached me and uttered a single word into my ear. "Cantaloupe," she whispered, and I had not a clue what she meant.

  It turned out that she was a professional speech coach working with actors and broadcasters. She told me that the best remedy for a crackling throat is a few slices of cantaloupe before speaking. Other melons will help, but nothing works quite like cantaloupe.

  I arrange to have some available, if possible, when I speak. It works like a charm and lasts longer than Hall's Mentho-Lyptus cough drops, which are my back up remedy.

- <u>Mac Frenzy.</u> Most conferences provide a PC as the default presentation computer but I produce my slides on my Mac. Occasionally, odd things happen to colors and graphics when you switch platforms. So I try to use my own laptop when I present. I bring along a little $20 dongle, that hitches my Mac to a PC VGA. I also bring a data key as a backup.

- <u>Stains Happen</u>. Somehow, things that spill will leap through the air to land on a speaker's blouse or suit jacket minutes before presentation. I always travel with an extra outfit for speaking which I bring in my backpack to the event. I usually choose dark clothes for the same reason.

- <u>The Unclickables</u>. If you like to walk around when you present, bring your own slide clicker and fresh batteries. Slides that don't advance precisely when you click can trip up your presentation timing. In fact, I recommend bringing two sets of double AAs. The TV clicker in your hotel room may not work either.

- <u>The Caller in the 3rd Row</u>. A speaker must remain reasonably gracious. But that does not mean you have to allow rudeness wreck your big moment. My pet peeve is the two folks who are chatting away close enough to the front of the room for me to hear while I'm speaking.

There is also the self-important executive who elects to take a call and proceeds to sit and chat in the room, usually with his hand cupped around his mouth as if that would mute his voice.

I give both situations about 20 seconds to self-resolve, then I stop speaking. I look at them with a slight smile on my face and then I wait. Pretty soon they realize that I'm staring at them.

Then, very politely, I say. "I hope you don't mind, but I'm trying to talk with these people, and I hate to compete with you." That usually solves the problem.

- The Crash/Bang Caterers. If you are the last speaker before a food break, caterers may be just outside your door oblivious to how their noise is encroaching on your milestone moment.

  It is entirely appropriate to ask someone to request they quiet down. It doesn't always solve the problem, but it sometimes helps.

- The Bellower Next Door. Sometimes you will be speaking in a room created by subdividing a larger room with a thin partition that does not block the noise.

I use this to illustrate that some things are beyond your control. In such situations you need to maintain good humor and do the best you can. Maintain grace under pressure. Showing annoyance to your audience is never a wise course.

Part 4
One Last Thing

19. The Fun Factor

Stellar Presentations is filled with paradoxes:

- I advocate simplicity, but spend much time describing the complexities of making a presentation.
- I tell you why Steve Jobs is the greatest presenter in tech industry history, but then urge you not to imitate him.
- I recommend that you speak in the first person present, yet you are presenting in order to launch something larger than yourself.
- I tell you to minimize using bullet points, yet here I am filling my last two chapters with bullet points.

Let me add one more paradox to the list.

- Have fun with it

Making a public presentation is damn hard. But if you really want to succeed, if you really wish to be stellar, then have as much fun as you possibly can while standing in front of the room.

Earlier, I commented that the value of fun in business is vastly underrated. In fact, fun is underrated almost everywhere.

Take education. As adults, we have come to understand there is a joy in learning. But how many of your grade school classes were fun? How much have you retained from the days when history required you to remember the dates but not the relevance of events?

Think about your most enlightening moments. Was it a fun? Yes, some learning comes from pain. But so much more is remembered and retained because the person who taught us enjoyed doing it and we enjoyed hearing or seeing it.

I would argue the same goes for our business experiences. Of course, we can't always do business, just with people whose company we enjoy. Some of it is hard-nosed and bare-knuckled. I will never find joy in a tax audit, for example.

But at the end of the day, the business relationships I've had that have continued for many years and through many transactions have been enjoyable.

The same goes for speaking. It's hard work and after more than 100 presentations I often still get apprehensive before I start.

But I do my best when I can get my head around making my presentation fun for me. My audiences respond better to me when I am enjoying my presentation. They remember what I say longer and it opens the door to many more business opportunities.

So have fun when you present. I'm serious about that.

And oh, I almost forgot: one last thing. If you had fun reading this book and you think you might have fun with me as your speaking coach or startup consultant please contact me: shelisrael1@gmail.com.

Afterword: About Me

First, and above all, I am a writer. I am at my happiest when I am putting words onto a computer screen as I am doing right now.

I was first paid to write when I was in high school and partly supported myself through college as a newspaper reporter. I've published two hardcover books and a Dow Jones ebook on social media and I've contributed freelance articles to BusinessWeek, Fast Company, Forbes magazine and numerous other publications.

 I've ghost written speeches and books for a few prominent people who I cannot mention.

I am at my most prolific when I am online. I have posted more than 1.5 million words in blogs since 2004, most of them on my current site, *globalneighbourhoods.net.*

Of particular value in preparing for *Stellar Presentations* were the four years during which I served as editor for *Conferenza Premium Reports*, an email newsletter that I co-founded in 2001. Conferenza's charter was to review tech conferences. Mostly, we watched speakers, reported on what they said, asked attendees their opinions and then told our readers what we thought.

We were the tech conference critics. In my job, I reviewed hundreds of conference speakers and got a sense of what worked and what didn't.

While writing has been my first passion, there is one part of it that I absolutely hate: the vow of poverty that is required of most writers throughout most of their careers.

My desire not to be homeless led me into a second career. In 1979, I became a tech sector communications consultant, mostly working for public relations agencies and overwhelmingly working with startup companies.

For seventeen years I owned and ran SIPR, a boutique PR firm based in Silicon Valley. Our specialty was first launches for startups.

As CEO, much of my time was spent helping entrepreneurs figure out what to say and how to help them get good at saying it.

It's not what PR agency CEOs usually do for clients, but I gave a great deal of energy to collaborating with entrepreneurs on what they should say to venture capitalists, the media and at launch presentations, because I felt that was the most important part of what my agency could do to help them get onto the playing field.

I was good at it. One year, my clients captured three of the nine Demo God Awards at the venerable DEMO conference. Other clients won many best of show awards at other events and more important to me, I would hear them tell their stories with words I helped them forge long after my work with them was completed.

After I sold off SIPR and co-launched Conferenza, I continued to serve as a speech coach for startups. I continue to do so, and I continue to enjoy how it helps entrepreneurs with great products and teams get past one of the earliest barriers on the startup's road to success—the initial presentation.

So, I thought that by virtue of being the conference speaker's critic and the startup speaker's coach, I was pretty damned good at the topic of stellar presentations.

But something happened in 2006 that vastly expanded my perspective on the subject. My friend, Robert Scoble, and I wrote a book called "*Naked Conversations*," about why businesses should embrace what we now call 'social media'.

It was widely acclaimed. I started getting requests for interviews by some of the press my agency used to pitch.

Then I started getting invitations to speak at conferences. I thought, with my background, that public speaking would be a breeze. It wasn't.

The first time I stepped onto a stage in front of a room filled with strangers and watched the lights dim, was the last time I can recall experiencing pure terror. I remember knocking knees and an incurably dry throat.

The feedback I received from my early talks told me that I did not quite suck, but I needed to get better. I started focusing on the tips that I had been giving my clients. I went back and read Conferenza reviews of other speakers.

Over time I got better. I came to understand the strategy of presentations as well as the little details that can gum up an otherwise good talk. And I became far more sensitive to the challenges of public speaking.

I have now been a keynoter more than 100 times. I've talked to students in South Africa, technologists in Ireland, bloggers in China, software entrepreneurs in India, government workers in Colombia and social media professionals in at least a dozen countries.

In fact, I have to admit that these days I like speaking almost as much as I like writing. They both incorporate one particular skill that seems to be at the core of everything I do professionally: storytelling.

Acknowledgements

To my wife Paula, who has endured, supported, edited and encouraged me into completing and publishing four books. She has put up with far more than I ever would have.

To my friend Harry Miller whose fine editing has made me look far more eloquent and literate than I actually am. I met Harry over 20 years ago when he was Editor at PC World Magazine, and I was a PR guy who had a few stories to tell. As editor, Harry uses a firm hand and a warm sense of humor.

To Ant Clay, who rescued me at deadline for this book by interrupting his weekend to compile the Table of Contents, a task that had impossibly confounded me. I first met Ant as @SoulSailor on Twitter, as I was completing my final draft of *Twitterville*. He shared a metaphor about the social being like a pub. I liked it so much that I restructured a chapter at deadline just so I could include it. The real treat was after all that, he endured hours on a train to have dinner with me one rainy London night. There's nothing like meeting an old friend for the first time.

To Michael Markman, who caught a small factual error in an earlier version of this book and corrected it online less than eight hours after I uploaded it to Kindle, showing me again how social media has improved my journalistic accuracy.

To the people I meet through social media, who inspire and inform me; who support and correct me; who are my toughest critics and most loving mentors.

And to Marjorie Furtado, the only grade school teacher who told me I could.

Made in the USA
Lexington, KY
03 April 2012